MINIBEASTS
Book 4

For pupils work...
Sue Palmer

Contents

Mini-verses	2
The Superslug	3
Yesterday the House was Full of Flies	6
Mini-maxims	7
Worms	8
Bookwormery	10
Ants on Display	13
The Star Queen	14
Monkey Business	16
It's a Small World	18
Letter-Bugs	20
Points of View: Big and Little	22
Spider's Surprise	24
Looking Glass Insects	29
Small is Beautiful	36
Creepy Crawly Visitors Book	37
Minibeasts and Dialect	38
Glossary	40
Jokes	back cover

'Who's that tickling my back?' said the wall.
'Me,' said a small
Caterpillar. 'I'm learning
To crawl.'

Ian Serraillier

There once was a boy of Baghdad,
An inquisitive sort of a lad,
He said, "I will see
If a sting has a bee,"
And he very soon found that it had.

Anon

Mini-verses

'Mother, oh mother! where shall we hide us?
Others there are in the house beside us –
Moths and mice and crooked brown spiders!'

James Reeves

A wasp on a nettle said: 'Coo!
We're in a right mess, me and you.
   We have got to sort out
   What this is about.
Please tell me – who's got to sting who?'

Frank Richards

God made the bees,
   The bees make honey.
      We do the work –
         The teachers get the money.

The Superslug

Mrs Potter was horrified when she found a slimy silvery trail in her sitting room. She spent the whole day tearing the room apart, hunting for snails. When the rest of the family came home she made them hunt too – until they managed to calm her down and she went off to make the tea.

All the time that Mrs Potter had been looking for a snail, the creature who had made the slime trail had been in hiding. He had watched and listened and waited, amazed at the commotion he had caused. Now that the Potters had had their tea, straightened out the sitting room, and gone off to bed, he breathed a great sigh of relief and crawled down from the underside of Mr Potter's chair.

He wasn't a snail at all.

He was a slug.

He was a small, neat, shiny brown slug with perfectly ordinary tentacles and a very extraordinary brain.

He was a slug genius: the Albert Einstein, the William Shakespeare and the Pablo Picasso of slugs, all wrapped into one. His name was Software.

But like all geniuses, he had some very odd ideas, as well as some clever ones.

His first odd idea was that he wasn't a slug at all, but a snail without a shell. He had tried out several empty snail shells in the garden, and even a seaside shell, but none of them seemed to fit. Besides, he didn't want just any old shell. He was hoping to find something special.

Then, one night, instead of making the usual excursion into the garden looking for food, Software had gone off to the family sitting room looking for a shell.

3

There he had seen the pouffe.

He admired its pork-pie plumpness, then he had his second odd idea.

"What a spiffing, spectacular shell that would make," he had said to himself. "A shell fit for a genius."

He had been about to try it out when Mrs Potter had walked into the room. Doubling his tracks to make sure he wasn't found, Software had been forced into hiding. There he had stayed ever since, dozing off every so often and missing all the talk about snails.

But now that all was quiet he had a chance to try again.

He knew that he wouldn't be disturbed for some time so he crept slowly back to the pouffe. It was pinky-red in colour with a warm, furry texture that tickled him as he walked. He crawled all the way up the side and to the top, then round, round, round he went, looking for a way in. Round, round, round, went a slimy, spiralling trail, all silvery in the streetlight that shone into the room.

But he couldn't find a way in.

By the time that morning came he was so tired that he had to give up. Besides, the family would soon be down for breakfast.

"Never mind," said Software to himself, "I shall try again tomorrow night," and he set off on the long crawl home.

Home was a hole next to the cellar, with a large colony of snails.

Snails do not like slugs. To a snail, a slug looks somehow naked, somehow not nice. Slugs give snails a bad name.

But because Software was a genius, the snails put up with him. Software did them favours, for he understood human talk. He gave them all the gossip. He told them beforehand exactly when a row of lettuces was being planned, and which strawberry beds had been scattered with poisonous pellets.

But Software did more than that. In listening to the human talk, he picked up some interesting words, which, translated into snail talk, made wonderful double-barrelled names. So a great big grandpa snail was called Slipper-sock, and a fat round grandma called Cat-Flap. There was a snail called Whole-Meal and another called Walkie-Talkie. The chief snail of all, with the very best name, taken from the talk of Tom Potter, was called User-Friendly. He had a wife called Floppy-Disc

and a son called Fast-Forward. It was the snails who chose 'Software' for Software.

Software also found names for the slugs that lived under the stones in the garden, like Gobstopper, Spittle and Slubber. This added to the comfortable feeling of superiority that the snails felt over the slugs, for not only did they have shells, they had names which were much more distinguished.

Nonetheless, they kept Software in his place. "He may be very useful," they said to each other, "but he mustn't get above himself."

They constantly reminded him of his shell-lessness. "You are not one of US! You are one of THEM!"

This had made Software ambitious. His sights were set very high. A pouffe for a shell! That would show User-Friendly!

Now he crawled his way to the edge of the carpet, across a stretch of polished floorboard, down a crack between them, along the ceiling of the cellar, through the entrance of the air vent, into The Hole that was home.

From *Software Superslug* by Joyce Dunbar

It was the perfect place for snails. It was hidden from the cellar by the air vent, and covered over in the driveway by a stone sink full of plants, so that nobody knew they were there. Warmth from the house and damp from the driveway created just the moist, humid conditions that snails like best. It was Software who had found it of course.

The snails were not yet asleep when Software arrived. "Well," they said, "what's new?"

"Oh nothing much today," said Software with a shrug. Then his eyes began to bulge and his body to boggle. "But just you wait," he said, trying to control his excitement, "I'll soon have something to show you." And he squashed himself up for a snooze.

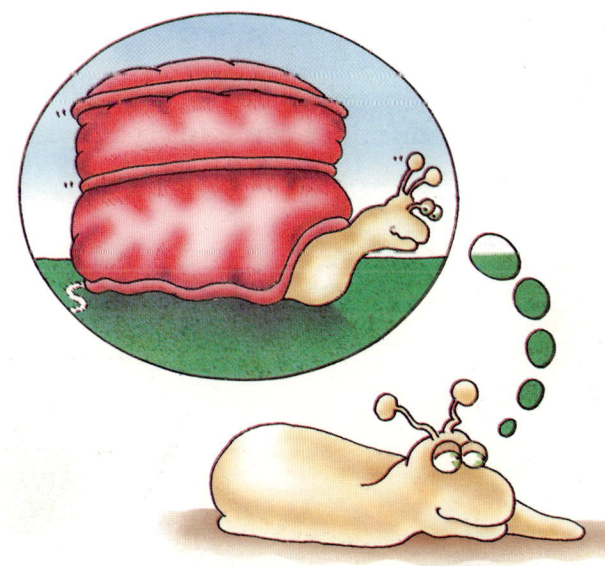

Yesterday the House was Full of Flies

One went spinning down the plughole,
Clinging to a tea-leaf.
Two pestered the dog. He snapped, and caught them.
He was as surprised as the flies.
Three sat all day on a fruit-loaf,
Disguised as currants.
Four zizzed in a spider's web,
Until the spider woke up.
Five chased each other round a lamp-shade
Until they were giddy.
Six padded up and down the windows,
And still can't fathom glass.
Seven sat on the warm electric kettle,
Until I switched it on.
Eight stuck to reading all about glue
In the fly-paper.
Nine played on a broken fly-swatter,
Laughing themselves silly.
Ten walked all over the mirror,
Admiring their stomachs.
Eleven pestered each other, trying to bark,
Doing an imitation of a dog-fight.
Twelve went supersonic into the window,
Knocked themselves out.
And hundreds just sat for hours,
Twiddling their legs.
I folded a paper, killed one,
And a thousand more came to its funeral.

Geoffrey Summerfield

A Worm Story

Peter Hatcher's family has moved to a new town – Princeton – for a year. Peter doesn't know anyone (apart, of course, from his four-year-old brother, Fudge, and his baby sister, Tootsie) and he's desperate to make a friend.

After almost two weeks of hanging around the house, I actually met a kid my age. He lives across the street, but he was at Scout camp when we first moved here. His name is Alex Santo and he's going into sixth grade too. He's very small, with hair that hangs into his eyes, and he's always wearing a T-shirt that says *Princeton, Class of '91*. By the time I met him, I was so lonely and bored I wouldn't have cared if he had three heads, as long as he was my age and wanted to be friends.

Alex came over one morning and said, "You want to go into business with me?"

"What kind of business?" I asked.

"Worms," he told me.

"Worms?" I asked.

"Yeah, worms," he said again.

"Worms!" Fudge said, jumping down the front steps. "Wormy wormy worms!"

Alex looked over at him.

"Don't mind him," I said. "He's just my little brother."

"Oh," Alex said. "So what do you say?"

"Sure," I told him, having no idea what kind of worm business Alex was talking about. "When do I start?"

"How about now?" Alex asked.

"Okay. What do I do?"

"First we dig them up. then we sell them to Mrs Muldour, down the street. She pays five cents a worm."

"What does she do with them?" I asked.

"She doesn't say. Some people think she uses them for fishing. Othe people think she uses them in her garden. Personally . . ." He stopped and scratched his head.

"Go on . . . go on . . ."

"I think she eats them," Alex said.

I thought for a minute. "Worm pie?"

"Yeah . . . and worm stew . . . and worm juice . . ."

"And worm soup," I said, getting warmed up. "And worm bread."

"Oh yeah, that's the best," Alex said. "Nice soft bread with little worms here and there . . ."

"You can make a really tasty worm and cheese sandwich on it," I said. We were doubled over now, laughing our heads off.

"And worm ice cream," Fudge said, jumping on top of us.

"Worm ice cream," Alex and I said together.

I decided that with Alex Santo in my class, Princeton might not be too bad.

That afternoon Alex and I went digging for worms. We rode our bikes over to the lake. It's easy to ride in Princeton because they have bike paths on every street. Alex had a pail and a couple of shovels and we got to work. Finding worms was no problem. An hour later we rode back to my house.

"Mrs Muldour likes her worms clean," Alex told me, turning on our hose.

"That figures, if she uses them for cooking," I said.

We left the pail of worms outside and went in for a drink. When we came out, Fudge was standing next to Tootsie's pram, dangling a worm in front of her.

"Cut that out!" I yelled, racing over to him.

"Why? she likes it," Fudge said. "Watch . . ."

Alex and I looked into Tootsie's pram. She laughed every time Fudge held up the worm.

"You're right," I said. "She does like it. Hey Mom . . . look at this!"

"What is it?" Mom called from where she was weeding Millie's organically grown vegetables.

"You've got to see for yourself," I called back.

She came over, wiping her hands on her jeans.

"Watch, Mommy," Fudge said, and he took the worm from behind his back and dangled it into Tootsie's pram.

She smiled and gurgled.

But Mom screamed. "Get that thing out of here. . . . Hurry up . . . get rid of it . . . now."

"It's just a worm, Mommy. Don't you like worms?"

"No, I don't. I really don't like worms at all. And I never want you to show me another one. Do you understand?"

Fudge put the worm on his arm and let it crawl up to his shoulder. "See . . . isn't he cute? I'm going to call him Willy. Willy Worm. And he'll be my very own pet. I'm going to sleep with him and he can eat next to me at the table and he'll take a bath with me . . ."

"Fudge!"

"Yes, Mommy?"

"I told you, I don't ever want to see that worm again. And you may *not* bring him into the house. And you may *not* hold him that close to Tootsie. Do you understand me this time?"

"You really don't like worms?" Fudge said.

"That's right," Mom said. "I really don't."

"Why not?" Fudge asked.

"It's nothing I can explain." Mom went back to weeding the garden. Fudge followed her.

"Is your family always like that?" Alex asked.

"You haven't seen anything yet!" I told him.

From *Super Fudge* by Judy Blume

Earth-worm

Do
you
squirm
when
you
see
an earth-worm?
I never
do squirm
because I think
a big fat worm
is really rather clever
the way it can shrink
and go
so small
without
a sound
into the ground.
And then
what about
all
that
work it does
and no oxygen
or miner's hat?
Marvellous
you have to admit,
even if you don't like fat
pink worms a bit,
how with that
thin
slippery skin
it makes its way
day after day
through the soil,
such honest toil.
And don't forget
the dirt
it eats, I bet
you wouldn't like to come out
at night to squirt
it all over the place
with no eyes in your face:
I doubt
too if you know
an earth-worm is deaf, but
it can hear YOU go
to and fro
even if you cut
it in half.
So do not laugh
or squirm
again
when
you
suddenly
see
a worm.

Leonard Clark

BOOKWORMERY

Well, the whole point of a library is to make it easy to find what you need. So the books are kept on the shelves in a special order. Non-fiction books are kept together in subject groups.

In most libraries each subject is given a number. Then the numbers are kept in order on the shelves, starting at 0 and going up to 1000.

THE DEWEY DECIMAL SYSTEM

- **000**   **General Sources of Information**
  e.g. computers, newspapers
- **100**   **Philosophy and Psychology**
  e.g. beliefs of ancient times
- **200**   **Religion**
  e.g. Christianity, Islam
- **300**   **Social Sciences**
  e.g. transport, fashion, customs, folklore
- **400**   **Language**
  e.g. English, Spanish, Urdu
- **500**   **Natural Science and Mathematics**
  e.g. maths, space, the earth, animals, plants
- **600**   **Science and Technology**
  e.g. engineering, farming and pets, cooking, buildings
- **700**   **The Arts and Hobbies**
  e.g. painting, music, theatre dance, sport
- **800**   **Literature**
  e.g. poetry, plays
- **900**   **Geography and History**
  e.g. places, famous people, the history of the world.

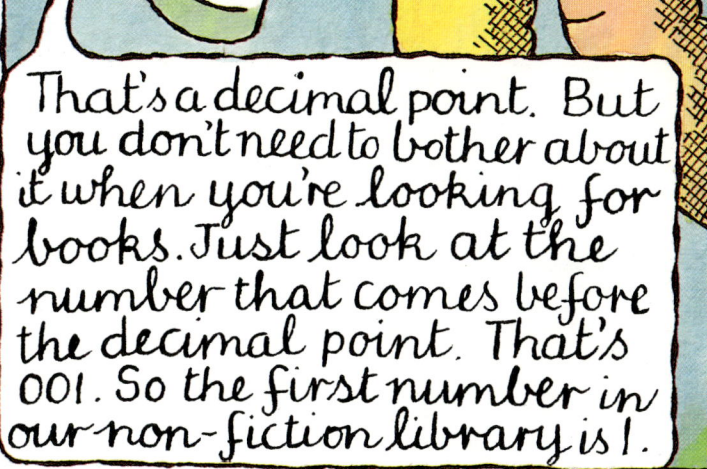

ANTS

by Jaswinder and Hannah

What are ants like?

Ants are insects so they have three segments called the head, the thorax and the abdomen. They have three pairs of legs (6) on the thorax and a pair of antenna on the head. Their jaws are called mandibles. Male ants have wings and so do queen ants, but ordinary female ants have no wings.

Ants

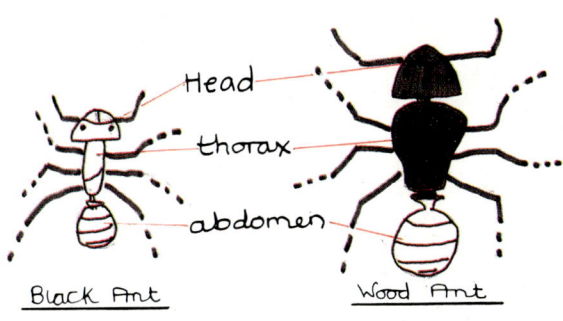

Black Ant   Wood Ant

Are there different sorts of Ants?

There are about 8,000 sorts of ants. Most of them live in very hot countries. In Britain there is the Black Ant, which is the sort of ant in our gardens. There is also the Wood Ant. It is bigger and it can bite and squirt acid. There is also the Medow Ant. It is brown and lives in humps in the fields. It keeps aphids like cows and milks them.

How do ants live?

Ants live in organised ways. They have a queen, who has all the babies. They have worker ants who look after the babies and hunt for food and do the work. Some worker ants are soldier ants with big heads and strong mandibles. The males are called drones and they don't do much. Ants feed on whatever is handy, but they like sweet things best.

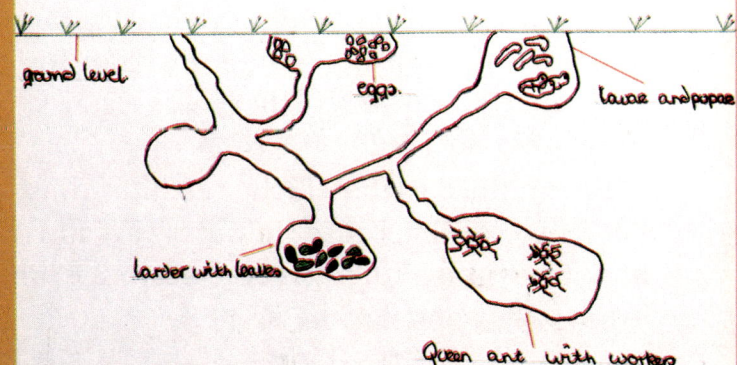

Cross section of an ant nest.
ground level — eggs — larvae and pupae — larder with leaves — Queen ant with workers

How are ants born?

The male ants mate with a queen and she lays eggs. She hides in the ground to bring up the babies and she feeds them on her spit. The eggs hatch into larvae, and the larvae turn into pupae. Ants hatch out of the pupae and come up to the ground to find food for themselves and the queen.

The Sting in the Tale?

THE STAR QUEEN

A folk tale from Africa

Once, long long ago, there were no insect pests in the world at all. No mosquitoes to bite men and buzz angrily about their heads, no flies to plague the animals and spread disease, no locusts to destroy crops and cause hardship and famine. The world was a much happier place, with food for everyone and hardly any illness.

In this wonderful time there was a young king who had everything he could want, except for a wife. He couldn't find anyone he loved enough to marry. One night when he was standing looking up at the stars, wishing he could find a bride, he saw one star which was much more beautiful than all the others. It seemed to be shining especially for him.

"If that star were a woman," the young king said sadly, "I should ask her to marry me."

Suddenly, the star seemed to swell, and its beams streamed down from the sky. There before him stood a beautiful girl, with hair as dark as the night and skin which shone like starlight.

"Who are you?" gasped the king.

"I am Nyachero, the daughter of the star. I was watching you as you were watching me, and I have persuaded my father to let me come down to earth."

"My wish has been granted." breathed the king, and he kneeled before Nyachero. "Will you marry me?" he asked.

The young girl nodded shyly, and went with the king back to his village so that preparations could be made for their wedding.

Nyachero and the king were married and were as happy as could be, except for one thing. Because Nyachero was a star's daughter, she could only come out at night. In the daytime she had to hide away, deep in a cave, because the sun's rays hurt her. The young king had to learn to see his bride only when darkness fell.

After a while, to everyone's delight, Nyachero found she was pregnant. In this country, women always returned to their own families when their babies were due to be born, so as the months went by she prepared to go back to her home in the sky to have her baby.

At last the time came, and the king gathered together twelve of his bravest men to escort Nyachero on her journey. But when she saw them Nyachero protested. "I must go alone," she said. "My star is different from your world. There are things there which your people might not understand."

"Nonsense," said the king firmly. "I will not have my queen travelling unaccompanied and, besides, I have many gifts for your father which they will carry for you."

At last the star-queen had to give in. "Very well," she said, "but they must promise not to touch anything while they are there. They must let the star-people look after them."

The bodyguards were made to promise, and the next night they went with Nyarchero and her king up to the top of a high mountain. Nyachero looked up to the sky. "Father," she cried, "send me a boat to carry me home."

As they watched, a beam of light shone down from the star, and a white boat came sailing slowly down it. Nyachero and her escorts climbed into the boat, and the king piled it high with gifts and kissed his bride goodbye. "Take care, my star-queen," he said softly. "Hurry back to me."

The boat sailed up into the sky for many hours. At last it landed in a strange twilight land and Nyachero asked the body-guards to help her out of the boat. There was no one there to greet them, so Nyachero led the men to a house. They went inside, past three large jars that looked like food containers, but here too it was deserted.

"Where is everyone?" asked one man. Nyachero looked out across the skies to the east. "On no," she cried, "please wait for me . . ." and she fled from the house. The men looked at each other in dismay . . . . .

The conclusion of this story is given in the Teacher's Book.

MONKEY BUSINESS

A Caribbean folk-tale

In the Caribbean, people tell stories of Anancy, the spider man. Sometimes Anancy was a man, sometimes he was a spider. As a spider, he was famous for his tricks. A spider may be smaller than other animals, but Anancy was clever and cunning, and he usually got his own way in the end. For instance, there was the time when Anancy was jealous of Monkey.

Long ago, Monkey was not the mischievous character he is today. He didn't copy other people's actions as modern monkeys do, or behave stupidly, or live in the trees. He lived a very sensible, sober life on the ground. He was always smartly-dressed, well-behaved and in control of every situation. All the other animals admired and respected him.

As time went on, Monkey became rather vain. Animals were always complimenting him on his appearance and his manners, so he began to strut around like a peacock, showing off to everyone. He became obsessed with his clothes, trying out all the latest fashions and parading around in them. Yet still the animals admired him. All except Anancy.

"Monkey's a show-off," Anancy said. "There's nothing all that special about him."

"Oh yes there is," said the others. "You're just jealous, that's all. Monkey is handsome and clever and smart – not like you."

"What do you mean, not like me?" said Anancy, jumping up and down with fury.

"Well, Monkey doesn't do stupid things like you," said the birds.

"Monkey doesn't jump up and down," said the rabbits.

Anancy was so angry he began to roll about on the ground.

"Monkey doesn't roll about on the ground," said the snake.

Anancy was beside himself. "You're all wrong," he yelled loudly. "You come here tomorrow and you'll see how wrong you are. You'll see Monkey jumping up and down and rolling on the ground. You'll see that he isn't handsome and clever and smart. He's stupid! He'll do anything I tell him."

The other animals laughed. "Don't be such a fool, Anancy," they said. "We'll come here tomorrow, but it won't be to see Monkey looking stupid – it'll be to laugh some more at you." And off they went, still giggling among themselves at how jealous Anancy was.

Now Anancy did not like being laughed at, so he thought up a plan. First he went and bought a very smart fashionable jacket. Then he made a number of holes in the jacket's lining. Then he went to a place he knew in the forest and spent some time scrabbling about among the anthills . . .

The next day, Anancy was sitting in his usual place in the forest waiting for his rival to pass by. Soon Monkey came strutting through the trees, looking as pleased with himself as ever, showing off his trendy clothes and good looks. The other animals saw him coming and waited with interest to see what would happen.

"Oh, Monkey," said Anancy. "I've been hoping to see you. I need your advice."

Monkey smiled condescendingly. "Yes, Anancy, and how can I help you?" he said.

Anancy brought out his new jacket. "It's this jacket," he said. "I've been invited to a party, and I want to wear it, but I'm not sure whether it's quite right. You know all about clothes, don't you, Monkey? What do you think?"

Monkey looked at the jacket. It certainly was a fine one, and he couldn't help admiring it.

"I don't know whether it'll suit me," said Anancy.

Monkey looked at the jacket again and then at Anancy and nodded understandingly.

"In fact, I think it'd look better on you than on me," Anancy added. Monkey smiled modestly. "On no, Anancy," he said.

"Yes it would," said Anancy. "Why don't you try it on?"

He knew Monkey wouldn't be able to resist. "Well, if you insist . . ." he said at last, and he took off his own jacket and climbed into Anancy's new one.

"You look great, Monkey," said Anancy, and the other animals agreed. So Monkey began strutting around, modelling the jacket, and Anancy watched, and waited . . .

The conclusion of this story is given in the teacher's book.

It's a Small World

The Microscope

Anton Leeuwenhoek was Dutch.
He sold pincushions, cloth, and such.
The waiting townsfolk fumed and fussed
As Anton's dry goods gathered dust.

He worked, instead of tending store,
At grinding special lenses for
A microscope. Some of the things
He looked at were:

      mosquitoes' wings,
the hairs of sheep, the legs of lice,
the skin of people, dogs, and mice;
ox eyes, spiders' spinning gear,
fishes' scales, a little smear
of his own blood,

      and best of all,
the unknown, busy, very small
bugs that swim and bump and hop
inside a simple water drop.

Impossible! Most Dutchmen said.
This Anton's crazy in the head.
We ought to ship him off to Spain.
He says he's seen a housefly's brain.
He says the water that we drink
Is full of bugs. He's mad, we think!

They called him *dumkopf*, which means dope.
That's how we got the microscope.

Maxine Kumin

Microworld

Imagine that you shrink into
      the micro-creatures' world
Then try to have a look inside
      each leaf that may be curled.
Inspect each growing thing you find
      with all the sprouting seeds,
Survey the living soil around,
      the ants and centipedes,
The bees that work on blossom trees,
      the weevils, water-skaters,
Ladybirds and butterflies,
      cicadas, bugs and slaters,
Mosquitoes, writhing millipedes,
      silkworms, gorging grubs,
The busy crowd of creatures here
      that dwell among the shrubs.

But wait . . . beware that web among the twigs
      and watch that spider's eyes.
Imagine that you grow again . . .
      become your normal size!

David Bateson

The Ant Explorer

Once a little sugar ant made up his mind to roam –
To fare away far away, far away from home.
He had eaten all his breakfast, and he had his Ma's consent
To see what he should chance to see and here's the way he went –
Up and down a fern frond, round and round a stone,
Down a gloomy gully where he loathed to be alone,
Up a mighty mountain range, seven inches high,
Through the fearful forest grass that nearly hid the sky,
Out along a bracken bridge, bending in the moss,
Till he reached a dreadful desert that was feet and feet across.
'Twas a dry, deserted desert, and a trackless land to tread;
He wished that he was home again and tucked-up tight in bed.
His little legs were wobbly, his strength was nearly spent,
And so he turned around again and here's the way he went –
Back away from desert lands feet and feet across,
Back along the bracken bridge bending in the moss,
Through the fearful forest grass, shutting out the sky,
Up a mighty mountain range seven inches high,
Down a gloomy gully, where he loathed to be alone,
Up and down a fern frond and round and round a stone,
A dreary ant, a weary ant, resolved no more to roam,
He staggered up the garden path and popped back home.

C. J. Dennis

> Dear ——
> When my family was having lunch, my Aunty found an ~~old insect~~ fly or something in her glass of wine. We dont know what it is and we want to know ~~its~~ WHERE FROM please ~~can~~ could you tell me and send it back
> Sincerely
> Yours Sinseerley
>
> creature   stamped address envelope

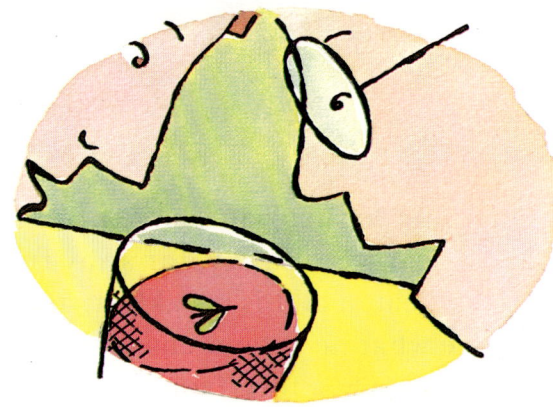

> 11 St George's Rd,
> Truro,
> Cornwall,
> TR1 3JE
> October 26th, 1991
>
> Dear Sir,
> My aunt found this creature in her glass of wine. The wine was from France and it was bottled in Doué, La Fontaine.
> I would like to know what the creature is but my family do not know. Please could you tell me? I should be grateful if you could send the creature back to me. I enclose a stamped addressed envelope.
> Yours sincerely
> Dan Hall.

THE NATURAL HISTORY MUSEUM

Mr Dan Hall
11 St George's Road
Truro
CORNWALL
TR1 3JE

Department of Entomology

Our ref
Enq91/808

Your ref

Date
4 November 1991

Direct line
071 938 8905

Facsimile
071 938 8937

Dear Dan

Thank you for your letter and the enclosed insect that you found in your aunt's glass of wine. The insect is a green lacewing (Neuroptera: Chrysopidae) called *Chrysoperla carnea* (Stephens); unfortunately it does not have an English name. It is the most common species of green lacewing in Britain and is most frequently seen in the autumn when it enters buildings to hibernate during the winter. At this time of year the colour of its body changes from bright green to pale brown. Your specimen may have fallen into the wine when it entered a cellar.

The adults feed on pollen and nectar but the larvae are fierce predators and eat greenfly, scaley insects and other soft-bodied insects that they find on the leaves and stems of plants. If you want to find out more about green lacewings I suggest you look them up in Michael Chinnery's book *A Field Guide to the Insects of Britain and Northern Europe* published by Collins.

Yours sincerely

Stephen Brooks

Points of View: Big and Little

Gulliver in Lilliput

I lay down on the grass, which was very short and soft, where I slept sounder than ever I remember to have done in my life, and as I reckoned, above nine hours; for when I awaked, it was just daylight. I attempted to rise, but was not able to stir: for as I happened to lie on my back, I found my arms and legs were strongly fastened on each side to the ground; and my hair, which was long and thick, tied down in the same manner. I likewise felt several slender ligatures across my body, from my armpits to my thighs. I could only look upwards, the sun began to grow hot, and the light offended mine eyes. I heard a confused noise about me, but in the posture I lay, could see nothing except the sky. In a little time I felt something alive moving on my left leg, which advancing gently forward over my breast, came almost up to my chin; when bending mine eyes downwards as much as I could, I perceived it to be a human creature not six inches high, with a bow and arrow in his hands, and a quiver at his back. In the meantime, I

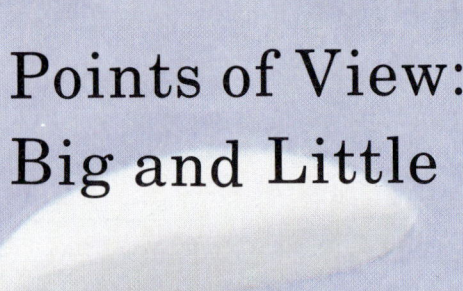

felt at least forty more of the same kind (as I conjectured) following the first. I was in the utmost astonishment, and roared so loud, that they all ran back in a fright; and some of them, as I was afterwards told, were hurt with the falls they got by leaping from my sides upon the ground. However, they soon returned, and one of them, who ventured so far as to get a full sight of my face, lifting up his hands and eyes by way of admiration, cried out in a shrill, but distinct voice, *Hekinab degul*: the others repeated the same words several times, but I then knew not what they meant. I lay all this while, as the reader may believe, in great uneasiness: at length, struggling to get loose, I had the fortune to break the strings, and wrench out the pegs that fastened my left arm to the ground; for, by lifting it up to my face, I discovered the methods they had taken to bind me; and, at the same time, with a violent pull, which gave me excessive pain, I a little loosened the strings that tied down my hair on the left side, so that I was just able to turn my head about two inches. But the creatures ran off a second time, before I could seize them.

Jonathan Swift

Gulliver in Lilliput

From his nose
Clouds he blows.
When he speaks,
Thunder breaks.
When he eats,
Famine threats.
When he treads,
Mountains' heads
Groan and shake;
Armies quake.
See him stride
Valleys wide,
Over woods,
Over floods.
Troops take heed,
Man and steed:
Left and right,
Speed your flight!
In amaze
Lost I gaze
Toward the skies:
See! and believe your eyes!

Alexander Pope

Spider's Surprise

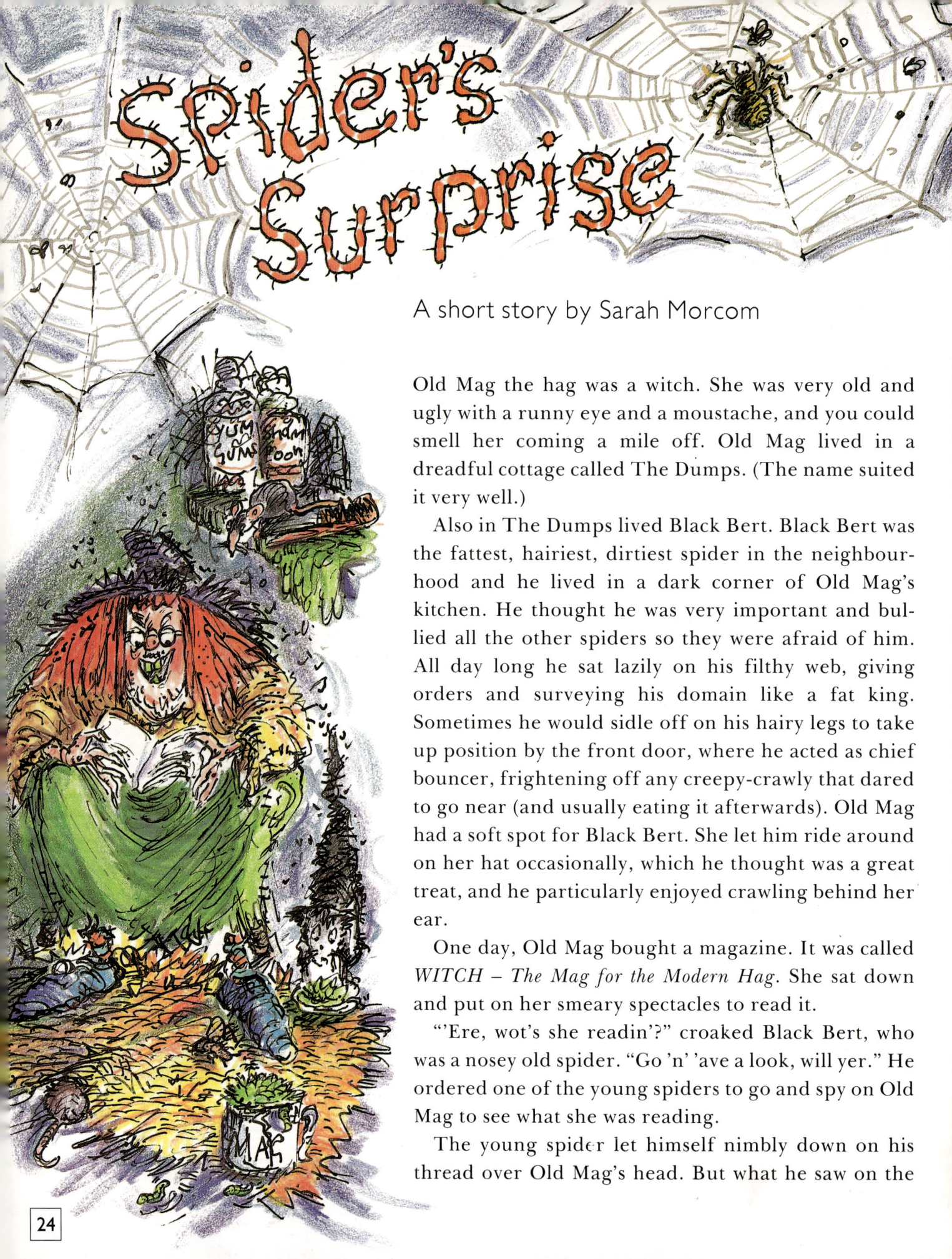

A short story by Sarah Morcom

Old Mag the hag was a witch. She was very old and ugly with a runny eye and a moustache, and you could smell her coming a mile off. Old Mag lived in a dreadful cottage called The Dumps. (The name suited it very well.)

Also in The Dumps lived Black Bert. Black Bert was the fattest, hairiest, dirtiest spider in the neighbourhood and he lived in a dark corner of Old Mag's kitchen. He thought he was very important and bullied all the other spiders so they were afraid of him. All day long he sat lazily on his filthy web, giving orders and surveying his domain like a fat king. Sometimes he would sidle off on his hairy legs to take up position by the front door, where he acted as chief bouncer, frightening off any creepy-crawly that dared to go near (and usually eating it afterwards). Old Mag had a soft spot for Black Bert. She let him ride around on her hat occasionally, which he thought was a great treat, and he particularly enjoyed crawling behind her ear.

One day, Old Mag bought a magazine. It was called *WITCH – The Mag for the Modern Hag*. She sat down and put on her smeary spectacles to read it.

"'Ere, wot's she readin'?" croaked Black Bert, who was a nosey old spider. "Go 'n' 'ave a look, will yer." He ordered one of the young spiders to go and spy on Old Mag to see what she was reading.

The young spider let himself nimbly down on his thread over Old Mag's head. But what he saw on the page nearly made him fall on to Old Mag's lap in fright. It read:

SPIDER SOUFFLÉ — A NEW REMEDY FOR THE AGEING WITCH
Capture your lost youth with this delicious tonic – tasty and effective – knocks years off your life!

INGREDIENTS
One fully-matured spider (as large and juicy as possible)
Two tablespoonfuls medium-sized spiders
½ teaspoon money spiders
6 pints slug slime . . .

The young spider read no further — he had seen enough to make him feel most uncomfortable. He quickly returned to Black Bert, quite sure they were going to be eaten.

"Nah, she ain't gonna cook us, stupid," growled Black Bert. "She'll use them imported ones from outside."

Black Bert sounded very sure, but underneath he was really quite frightened, because they all knew that imported spiders were thought to be tough and tasteless.

The next day, further alarming things began to happen. Old Mag seemed to be in a very strange mood. She pottered round the cottage tidying things up, and even dusted away some of the larger cobwebs. Black Bert was furious at this disturbance to his filthy home. At tea time Old Mag did something unbelievable for her — she washed her hair! I won't tell you what sort of things came out of it into the water (it might put you off your next meal), but the sink was blocked for days afterwards. Then the spiders watched, amazed, as she laid the table for two with her best black china and a vase of deadly nightshade and stinkweed as a centrepiece. That evening a young, rather greasy-looking wizard called at The Dumps, and he and Old Mag sat down to a candle-lit dinner. They leered at each other and held hands across the table, and Black Bert didn't like it one bit.

Over the next few days the young wizard visited very often. Old Mag seemed to have forgotten about

Black Bert altogether. She no longer asked him to ride on her hat and instead spent all her time dressing up and making herself look fancy for her wizard boyfriend. All this put Black Bert in a nasty temper and he took it out on the younger spiders, making their lives a daily misery.

Then, one morning, one of Black Bert's spies came rushing to him in a state of extreme panic. "She's got the spider recipe out again and the pot's already on the boil. We're done for now!"

Black Bert thought quickly. "All right you lot, keep yer 'eads on. This calls for Emergency Operations. Go 'n' get the Black Box an' don't mess about!"

Only Black Bert knew what was in the Black Box. On it was printed TOP SECRET in large letters. Black Bert took a rusty old key and opened it up. Inside was a large package marked CAUTION: OPEN IN EMERGENCY ONLY. With the package was a dirty sheet of paper covered with spidery writing. It read:

SPIDER SUPERGLUE: THE ULTIMATE DEFENSIVE WEAPON FOR SPIDERS

Instructions for making superglue:
1 Eat as much of enclosed confectionery as possible.
2 Spin webs in normal way.

Black Bert ripped open the parcel and there, in a sticky, glistening pile, was an enormous quantity of wine gums.

"Right, mates," said Black Bert. "Get stuck into this lot and FAST!"

Immediately the pile of wine gums was covered with a wriggling mass of spiders, all tearing and chomping at the sweets. Black Bert sat in the middle, dribbling and smacking his lips in an unsavoury manner. When they'd finished, the spiders felt very full, and extremely sticky.

"Now then, comrades," said Black Bert with a loud belch. "Back to your stations and get spinnin'!"

Meanwhile Old Mag was getting the pot nice and hot for the Spider Soufflé. She read the recipe out loud to herself: "One fully-matured spider – Ah yes . . ."

She went over to the dark corner where Black Bert lived, with a nasty smile on her face. "Bertie! Bertie, darling. How would you fancy a little ride on Auntie Mag's hat today? Come out, dearie, and say hello to your Auntie."

Black Bert bounced back into the shadows, grinning a horrible grin. Old Mag poked at him with her finger and immediately a mass of sticky web stuck to it. (Black Bert's web was made of Spider superglue!)

Old Mag pulled the curtain aside and got quite a shock – the curtain stuck to her hand! She pulled hard but it wouldn't budge.

Old Mag stamped her foot and muttered some nasty words under her breath. Finally she gave a great yank and brought the curtain pole clanging down. She fell back on to a chair, cursing and grumbling, and in his corner, Black Bert sat smiling and rubbing his hairy front legs together in quiet satisfaction.

Meanwhile, the other spiders had been weaving their superglue webs with great speed all over the kitchen, covering every piece of furniture they could find. So when Old Mag tried to get up, she found the chair stuck firmly to her bottom. At that moment, the doorbell rang and Black Bert slunk away to answer it. It was Old Mag's boyfriend and he was just in time to see Old Mag give a last, furious tug at the chair,

ripping her skirt off with it. There she stood in her baggy, black bloomers, showing her horrible, warty legs. I'm afraid to say she looked so ridiculous that the wizard couldn't stop himself laughing.

Old Mag was so angry it looked as if she would burst – her face was purple. "Get out!" she screamed at the wizard. "Get out! And you needn't come back again!"

Then she turned to Black Bert. "I think this is all your doing, you creepy little insect. Get rid of this stuff immediately or I'll turn you into – into—"

"Spider Soufflé?" said Black Bert with a leery smile. "That's wot you was goin' to turn us all into, wasn't it, *dear* Auntie Mag? And until you promise to leave us alone an' treat us respec'ful-like, I'm afraid you'll 'ave a sticky time of it."

"All right, I promise, I promise," said Old Mag, dragging the rug with her. (She's stuck to that now.)

By the time all the spiders had mixed the special paste to unstick the superglue, Old Mag looked like a walking scrapyard, with half her kitchen stuck to her. She didn't get rid of the wizard as quickly as she would have liked either, for in trying to get out, he'd stuck to the doorhandle.

So that is how Black Bert showed Old Mag he was not going to be made into Spider Soufflé and ruled the kitchen once more. Mag went back to her old, dirty ways again, but she was always very polite to any spider she saw, for fear of meeting a sticky end!

LOOKING GLASS INSECTS

Characters

Narrator 1
Narrator 2
Alice
The Red Queen
A railway guard
A goat
A beetle
A horse
A gnat
A rocking horse fly
A snapdragon fly
A bread and butter fly

Scene One: The Looking Glass World

Narr. 1   When Alice stepped through the looking glass

Narr. 2   into the Looking Glass World,

Narr. 1   everything was very strange indeed.

Narr. 2   It was back to

Narr. 1   front,

Narr. 2   and topsy-

Narr. 1   turvy! For a start Looking Glass writing is

Narr. 2   the wrong way round.

Narr. 1   You have to hold it up to a mirror before you can read it.

Narr. 2   And even then it doesn't usually make much sense.

JABBERWOCKY

'Twas brillig, and the slithy toves
Did gyre and gimble in the wabe:
All mimsy were the borogoves,
And the mome raths outgrabe.

Narr. 1 Another thing about the Looking Glass World is that if you want to get somewhere,

Narr. 2 you have to walk in the opposite direction!

Narr. 1 It's all rather like stepping into a dream.

Alice This is all rather like stepping into a dream.

Narr. 2 For instance, Alice found the pieces from a chess set had come to life.

Alice I found the White King and the White Queen arguing in the sitting room.

Narr. 1 When she went for a walk in the garden, she saw the Red Queen,

Narr. 2 who had grown to human size and was strolling among the flowers.

Alice The Red Queen! I think I'll walk over there to meet her.

Narr. 1 You can't possibly do that.

Alice Why not?

Narr. 2 You'd be much better walking the other way.

Alice But it's silly to walk the other way. I'm going in the wrong direction – oh!

(She bumps into the Red Queen)

Red Q. Oh! Where have you come from? And where are you going? Look up, speak nicely and don't twiddle your fingers all the time.

Alice If you please, ma'am I was walking in the garden and I think I've lost my way.

Red Q. Lost your way? I don't know what you mean by *your* way. All the ways about here belong to me. But why did you come out here at all? Curtsey while you're thinking what to say — it saves time. Open your mouth a little wider when you speak, and always say "Your majesty".

Alice I wanted to see the Looking Glass World, your majesty.

Red Q. Well then, why didn't you say so? Come with me, child.

Narr. 1 The Red Queen led Alice down a path.

Narr. 2 And they soon found themselves up on top of a hill.

Red Q. Here we are. Look all you want.

Alice Oh, it's lovely. But why is the countryside all split up into squares?

Narr. 1   Alice could see lots of little brooks running *across* the countryside.

Narr. 2   And lots of green hedges running up and down.

Narr. 1   So it was all criss-

Narr. 2   crossed.

Alice   I declare it's marked out like an enormous chess board! Yes, it's a great huge game of chess being played all over the world. Oh, what fun! How I wish I could join in.

Red Q.   That's easily managed. You may be a white pawn if you like.

Alice   Oh yes please, your majesty!

Red Q.   Do you know how to play? A pawn starts on the second square – that's where we are now. You can move across two squares in your first move, so you'll have to go very quickly through the third square – by railway, I should think. Then into the fourth square, and the other pieces will show you the way after that. Are you ready?

Alice   Oh yes, your majesty.

Red Q.   Then speak in French if you don't know the English for a thing, turn out your toes when you walk, and remember who you are. Oh, and look out for insects.

Alice   Insects?

Red Q.   Looking Glass Insects. They're all over the place between the third and fourth squares. Goodbye.

Alice   Goodbye. Goodness, I wonder what sort of insects. I hope they don't sting. But there's no point in worrying about it – everything's so strange here anyway. Now here's a little brook. If I jump over it, I should be in the third square and I can start my move.

Narr. 2   Remember to jump backwards!

Scene Two: The third square

Narr. 1   As soon as Alice jumped over into the third square, she found herself in a railway carriage.

Narr. 2   A Looking Glass Railway Carriage, where everything is like a bad dream!

Narr. 1   The other passengers were a goat, a beetle, and a horse.

Narr. 2   And the guard was very bad-tempered.

Guard   Tickets please!

Goat	Here's mine.
Beetle	And mine.
Horse	And mine.
Guard	Now then, show your ticket, child.
Alice	I'm afraid I haven't got a ticket. There wasn't a ticket office where I came from.
Guard	Don't make excuses. You should have bought a ticket from the engine driver.
Narr. 1	The guard looked at Alice, first through a telescope
Narr. 2	then through a microscope.
Guard	You're travelling the wrong way.
Goat	So young a child ought to know which way she's going, even if she doesn't know her own name.
Beetle	She ought to know her way to the ticket office even if she doesn't know her alphabet.
Horse	She'll have to go back from here as luggage,
Goat	Or by post,
Beetle	Or pull the train herself the rest of the way.
Horse	Or change engines . . . *(he chokes)*
Alice	Oh dear, how hoarse you are!
Narr. 1	Then Alice heard a little voice in her ear.
Gnat	You might make a joke about that, you know. Something about 'horse' and 'hoarse'.

Narr. 2　But she couldn't see anyone at all.

Guard　I advise you take a return ticket every time the trains stops.

Alice　Oh, how silly. Indeed I shan't. I don't belong on this railway journey at all – it's just to get me very quickly through the third square. I was in a wood just now and I wish I could get back there.

Gnat　You might make a joke about that too. Something about I would if I could.

Alice　Who *is* that talking? And if you're so anxious to have a joke made, why don't you make one yourself?

Gnat　(*sighing deeply*) Don't be unkind. You are my friend, a dear friend and an old friend. And you won't hurt me, even though I am an insect.

Alice　Oh, you're an insect. Is that why I can't see you? (*Anxiously*) What kind of insect are you?

Narr. 2　But before the little voice could answer, the Guard spoke again.

Guard　Keep your seats, please! The train is just about to jump over a brook.

Alice　Oh good. That'll take us into the fourth square. Maybe I'll get out of this train.

Narr. 1　And at that moment the carriage rose straight up in the air.

Alice　OOOOOh!

Goat
Beetle
Horse
Guard　} OOOOOOoooooooooh. (*their voices fade away*)

Scene Three: Looking Glass Insects

Narr. 1　Alice found herself sitting under a tree.

Narr. 2　Beside her was an enormous gnat.

Gnat　What do you mean – what sort of insect? Don't you like all insects?

Alice　Are you the little voice?

Gnat　I'm a gnat. Don't you like all insects?

Alice　Er . . . well, I like them when they can talk. None of them ever talk where I come from.

Gnat　Really? What sort of insects do you rejoice in where you come from?

Alice	I don't rejoice in insects at all, because I'm rather frightened of them – at least the large kinds. But I can tell you the names of some of them.
Gnat	Do they answer to their names?
Alice	I don't think so.
Gnat	What's the use of their having names if they won't answer to them?
Alice	No use to *them*, but it's useful to the people that name them, I suppose. If not, why do things have names at all?
Gnat	I can't say. However, go on with your list of insects. You're wasting time.
Alice	Well, there's the horsefly.
Gnat	All right. Here in Looking Glass World, we have the rocking horse fly.
R.H. fly	(*Appearing from behind a bush*) **Good afternoon.**
Alice	Goodness! Who are you?
R.H. fly	I'm called the rocking horse fly because I'm made entirely of wood and I get about by swinging from branch to branch.
Alice	What do you live on?
R.H. fly	Sap and sawdust.
Alice	You look very bright and sticky.
R.H. fly	I've just been repainted. Do you like it?
Goat	It's lovely. Go on with your list of insects.
Alice	Well, there's the dragonfly.
Gnat	Ah, here we have the snapdragonfly. Do you know the game of Snapdragon that's sometimes played at Christmastime?
Alice	Yes. My father throws raisins into a bowl of brandy and sets them alight. Then the other grownups have to scoop the raisins out and eat them.
Gnat	Then meet the snapdragon fly.
S.D. fly	(*crawling over to Alice*) **My body is made of plum-pudding, my wings of holly leaves, and my head is a raisin burning in brandy.**
Alice	How lovely. And what do you live on?
S.D. fly	Frumenty and mince-pies. And I make my nest in a Christmas box.

Alice   It must be very difficult with your head on fire. I wonder if that's the reason some insects are so fond of flying into candles – because they want to turn into snapdragon flies!

Gnat   What other insects do you have?

Alice   Let's see, there's the butterfly.

Gnat   Ah, in Looking Glass World we have the bread and butter fly. There's one crawling at your feet.

Alice   So there is.

B.&B. fly   My wings are thin slices of bread and butter, my body is a crust, and my head is a lump of sugar.

Alice   And what do *you* live on?

B.&B. fly   Weak tea with cream in it.

Alice   But supposing you can't find any.

B.&B. fly   Then we die of course.

Alice   But that must happen very often.

B.&B. fly   It always happens.

Alice   Oh dear.

Gnat   I think that's enough Looking Glass Insects for one day.

Alice   Yes, I think it is. I'd better get on across the fourth square or I'll miss my move.

Gnat   You could make a joke about that, you know. You're a miss, and you'll miss your move.

Alice   Why do you want me to make jokes about everything? And such very bad jokes too.

Gnat   AAaaaaahhhh

Narr. 1   And the Looking Glass Gnat sighed so deeply that he sighed himself away.

Alice   What's the point of making jokes, if it makes him so unhappy?

Narr. 2   But, then, this is the Looking Glass World . . . and everything's back

Narr. 1   to front

Narr. 2   and topsy

Narr. 1   turvy.

Small is Beautiful

Dragonfly

Over the pond
where the children play
I saw somebody
strange, today:
a slender, glittering,
trembling thing
with stuff like cellophane
on its wing

It wasn't a butterfly
or bee
lolloping, blundering
loose and free
it darted here
and it darted there
like a quivering firework
in the air

Down by the pond
I stared, and stood
in the heat of the morning.
I wished it would
stay and settle
but it went by
burning, beautiful
dragonfly

Jean Kenward

The Gnats

The gnats are dancing in the sun,
In vibrant needles of light they run
On the air, and hover in noiseless sound,
Ecstasy ballet, round and around,
Soon for human body bound.

The pin-thin slivers, wingy, white,
Whirl in restless, passionate flight–
Zooming atoms circling, twisting,
Darting, jiving,
Target-diving.
In orbit on orbit of dazzle-gold light,
The gnats are limbering up to bite.

Odette Tchernine

Ladybird

Tiniest of turtles!
Your shining back
Is a shell of orange
With spots of black

How trustingly you walk
Across this land
Of hairgrass and hollows
That is my hand

Your small wire legs,
So frail, so thin,
Their touch is swansdown
Upon my skin

There! break out
Your wings and fly
No tenderer creature
Beneath the sky

Clive Sansom

St. Petroc's School Creepy Crawly Visitors' Book

The pupils of St. Petroc's School kept a record on the computer of all the minibeasts they could find within the school grounds. At the end of the project they made it into a "Visitors' Book".

```
Name of visitor:  centipede
Place found:      the path to school under a loose stone
Finder(s):        Julie, Oonah, Kylie
Date:             12th July
Description:      very small and thin, yellowish,
                  wriggling.  We counted its legs and we
                  could only count 56.  It had segments.
```

Facts about the visitor
Centipede means 100 legs. It is not an insect because it has more than three segments and more than six legs. They only come out at night.

```
Name of visitor:  pond skater
Place found:      on surface of school pond
Finder(s):        Patrick, Andy B.
Date:             12th July
Description:      Quite a thin body with six long legs
                  that move about on the top of the
                  water.  Quite small.  There were a lot
                  of them together under the branches
                  near the edge of the pond.
```

Facts about the visitor
One book calls it a water strider and another one calls it a water skater.

```
Name of visitor:  froghopper bug
Place found:      school field
Finder(s):        Stephen, Marie
Date:             13th July
Description:      It was inside cuckoo spit on a long
                  piece of grass.  The cuckoo spit was
                  like white soapy bubbles.  The frog
                  hopper bug is very small and green and
                  it is hiding in the bubbles.
```

Facts about the visitor
The cuckoo spit is to keep the bug wet. The bug is the frog hopper larva.

We do not usually *write* in local or ethnic dialects. It is important that written English should be easy for all English speakers to read and understand, no matter where they come from. For this reason, there is one English dialect which should always be used for written English. It is called "Standard English".

You can speak in a standard dialect too. The people who read the news and weather forecasts on TV and radio always speak Standard English, so that everyone can understand, all over the country.

A tarantula spider was found in a health club in Cardiff. No one knows how the spider came to be there, but police are assuming it has escaped from a collection. It appeared to be enjoying the sauna.

Sometimes poets like to use dialect in poems. John Agard is a poet with a Caribbean background. He sometimes writes poems in "Black English" dialect. This one is based on an old proverb.

Early Bird Does Catch The Fattest Worm

Late again
going to be late again
for school again
and I can't say
I overslept
can't blame it
on the bus
can't blame it
on the train
can't blame it
on the rain
and Granny words
buzzing in my brain
'Early bird does catch the worm'
and I thinking
Teacher going tell me off
and I wishing
I was a bird
and teacher was a juicy worm.

John Agard

Glossary

♦ **abbreviation** (n.)
A short way of writing something, often using initials,
e.g. *e.g. = for example*
i.e. = that is
Mr = Mister.

♦ **accent** (n.)
The way a person pronounces words – it is affected by tone of voice and speech **rhythms**. Accents vary from one part of the country to another, and the same words can sound different if spoken in different accents.
   Particular accents sometimes go with particular dialects of English.

♦ **adverbs** (n.)
[See also **part of speech**]
A word which describes an action
e.g. *quickly, slowly, noisily.*

♦ **apostrophe** (n.)
A **punctuation mark** like a flying comma. It shows
1. where letters have been missed out of a word or words, e.g.
   it'll = it will
   can't = cannot
2. ownership, e.g. *Anancy's jacket, Mrs Potter's house*

♦ **catalogue** (n.)
A list of items arranged in a special order so that they can be found quickly.
[See also: **index, classification, databank**]

♦ **to classify** (v.)
To arrange items in order.
classification (n.)
A system for arranging items in order, e.g.
the Dewey Decimal Classification System

♦ **comma** (n.)
A punctuation mark used between the items in a list, or to separate parts of a sentence.

♦ **databank** (n.)
Information about a particular subject **classified** and stored for reference on a computer.

♦ **dialect** (n.)
A way of speaking the language which is particular to one part of the country. There are dialect words (such as 'emmet' for 'ant') and dialect grammars (such as 'We was there' for 'We were there').
   Dialects often have an **accent** which go with them.
[See also **Standard English**]

♦ **direct speech** (n.)
The actual words someone speaks, as shown in a piece of writing.
[See also **speech marks**]

♦ **encyclopedia** (n.)
A book or set of books giving information on many subjects

♦ **exclamation mark** (n.)
A punctuation mark (!) which shows that a phrase or sentence
1. should be spoken in a raised voice, e.g.
   "Help! Fire!"
or
2. is used in a joking or unusual way:
   "Old Mag nearly met a sticky end!"

♦ **folktale** (n.)
A story which has been handed down from one generation to another. Folktales are usually a spoken tradition i.e. they are told, not written down.

♦ **indent** (v.)
   Begin your writing a little way in from the margin, to show that you are starting a new **paragraph** (as we have done in the first line of this definition).

♦ **index** (n.)
An alphabetical list, which shows the subjects dealt with in a book, a set of encyclopaedias, or a whole library.
[See also **catalogue**]

♦ *italic print* (n.)
A type of print which leans towards the right. It is used to draw attention to particular words. The most common reasons for the use of italic print are:
1. for the titles or books, films, etc.
2. to show that a word should be **stressed** when read aloud.

♦ **joining word** (n.phr.)
[See also **part of speech**]
A word which joins words or groups of words together, e.g. and, but, when, so, as, while, because, although.

♦ **limerick** (n.)
A type of verse (usually funny), which has two rhyming lines, then two shorter rhyming lines, and a last line which rhymes with the first two.